St Andrews
Through Time and Tide

Lorn Macintyre & Peter Adamson

First published in the United Kingdom in 2017 by Alvie Publications,
52 Buchanan Gardens,
St Andrews,
Fife KT169LX.
Tel: 01334 475227

Printed and bound in Warsaw by Hussar Books

Acknowledgements

Grateful thanks to the following for their assistance.

Catherine Stihler, for her generous Foreword. For the use of honorary graduate photographs, the University of St Andrews. For the section on the Sciences at the University of St Andrews: Professor David O'Hagan, School of Chemistry; Professor Graham Turnbull, School of Physics and Astronomy; Professor Jim Naismith, School of Biology; Andrew Cole, Administrative Assistant (Teaching), School of Biology; Professor David Crossman, Dean of Medicine; Dr Phil Irving, Science Manager, Sea Mammal Research Centre. Alan Richardson. Alison Miller, Thomas Marr, and Gaby Levey, for photographic advice. Mandy Peden, for her cooperation and that of her three horses. Stuart Cameron, for guidance on setting the book. Kinburn Museum, for help with photographing artefacts. C. Morris, S.M.R.U. and M. Arso, S.M.R.U. for their photographs. Kenneth Fraser, Erica Hollis and Mary Macintyre for their textual advice and proofreading.

Dedication

This book is dedicated by Peter Adamson to his grandsons: Henry, Oliver, Orran, Finlay and Innis.

Foreword

The talents of Peter Adamson and Lorn Macintyre are once again on display in this exquisite book of photography. Peter and Lorn have a very special place in the life of the town and this new book encapsulates so much of the essence of St Andrews. From the sheer physical beauty of medieval ruins to simple day to day life, from lab work to May dip, from seagulls to the joy of Jannettas' ice cream, St Andrews is immortalised through this work where photographs and words combine to tell the story of this unique place. Whether you live in the town or studied at the University, this book, of what appears at first glance as lovely photographs, on a second glance you discover a different meaning, something you missed which adds again to the sophistication of this art work; each photograph has a place, a time, a story. Each one of us who has been touched by the town and the University knows that through these photographs your own St Andrews experience can be re-told. No season escapes their notice and the honesty of their work is what resonates. I hope you enjoy this book as much as I have and when not in St Andrews you can open it up and feel that you are once again back in the town which will always touch you no matter where you are in the world.

Catherine Stihler
Alumnus and Rector of the University of St Andrews
Member of the European Parliament for Scotland

4

Pilgrims approaching St Andrews would have welcomed the sight of spires and towers after a long journey barefooted, or in cumbersome sandals.

The sun is setting at the end of a day to be remembered, with the bride's dress trailing on the stonework of the old pier, and the harbour at peace after another busy day. The trinity of towers on the horizon adds harmony.

Mandy Peden, expert horsewoman, is a regular rider on the West Sands, usually in the early morning before the world awakes. In this dynamic shot, with St Andrews in the background, she rides Magic, with the frisky Oz on her right, the more docile Mia on her left.

A ruminative stroll in sunlight by the sombre ruins of the Cathedral.

The effigy of Saint Andrew in the Town Hall on the carved wooden panel is believed to have come originally from Holy Trinity Church. Boars roamed the area in times past, as the local place name of Boarhills records. The number 1115 at the base is an enigma, since the panel is not a twelfth century creation. Did it replace an older version?

In the perfumed peace of the Botanic Garden, Saint Andrew lugs his X shaped cross towards immortality. The Galilean fisherman abandoned his nets to become a disciple of Christ, but his spreading of the gospel beyond Palestine was cut short cruelly by crucifixion at Patras in Greece. Saint Rule brought relics of Andrew to the Scottish coastal settlement which bears Andrew's name with pride. A bodily relic of Saint Andrew is preserved in St James' Roman Catholic Church, The Scores, St Andrews.

St Andrews Cathedral was founded in 1162 by Arnold, Abbot of Kelso. It was the largest church in Scotland, originally measuring in its whole length over 121 metres, but later reduced after the collapse of the west front circa 1272 to the present overall length of over 113 metres. Nevertheless it was still a massive and magnificent structure when, that day in July 1318, the horse bearing Robert the Bruce to his coronation clattered up the aisle to the altar, one of several in the sacred building.

But in 1559 the riders who arrived in St Andrews weren't there to worship.

> And wi' John Calvin i' their heads,
> And hammers i' their hands and spades,
> Enraged at idols, mass and beads,
> Dang the Cathedral down....
> M.W. Tennant.

This is poetic licence, since the demolition of the Cathedral seems to have occurred over several decades.

And still endure, and still decay,
Towers that the salt winds vainly beat.
Ghost-like and shadowy they stand
Clear mirror'd in the wet sea-sand.

From 'Alma Matres' by Andrew Lang.

Lang was one of the most famous graduates of the University of St Andrews, a prolific author, including several popular anthologies of fairy stories.

A dramatic view of the Cathedral from St Rule's Tower, the traditional name given to the early twelfth century church which preceded the present Cathedral.

The prospect of South Street from the top of St Rule's Tower.

The tombstones and funerary monuments in the atmospheric churchyard within the Cathedral precincts are mainly from the eighteenth and nineteenth centuries, though some graves still receive flowers in remembrance.

Each July New Dawn in Scotland holds a Catholic Pilgrimage Conference in St Andrews, including Mass in the ruins of the Cathedral. Always well attended by all ages, including townspeople, the Mass recreates the piety of the Cathedral before it was wrecked.

The atmospheric silhouette of St Andrews Castle, scene of riotous living and murder. The English ambassador wrote in wonder that James Beaton, Archbishop of St Andrews, who lived in the Castle from 1523 to 1539, 'gave livery nightly to twenty-one score horses.' The Archbishop's nephew Cardinal Beaton did not fare so well. In 1546 he was murdered by Protestants (possibly encouraged by Henry VIII for political reasons) and his body was hung from a wallhead. Thereafter the assassins and their supporters were besieged in the Castle for a year. The Scottish army was unable to take it until reinforcements arrived from France.

The ruins of St Andrews Castle date from the sixteenth century. However, an older castle on the site was erected circa 1200 by Bishop Roger, who required a residence (with exceptional views) befitting the nearby Cathedral's chief dignitary. The Wars of Independence were traumatic, with the castle captured and recaptured, demolished and rebuilt. Following the Battle of Bannockburn, the Scottish nobles could toast their victory in the Castle's Great Hall.

Why does the sea moan evermore?
Shut out from heaven it makes its moan,
It frets against the boundary shore;
All earth's full rivers cannot fill
The sea, that drinking thirsteth still.
    Christina Georgina Rossetti.

The sombre silhouette of Martyrs' Monument, appropriately atmospheric because it commemorates some of the Protestant martyrs executed in St Andrews between 1528 and 1560 in the pitiless violence towards people and property during the period of religious conflict which culminated in the Scottish Reformation. The monument was erected in 1842-43 by public subscription. Inevitably eroded by salt-laden North Sea winds, it was restored by public appeal in 2013.

The most famous golf course in the world requires constant attention. Divots left by clubs are treated, and water is swept into the Swilken Burn so that play can commence.

Too misty to tee-off? Royal & Ancient members can watch for the weather to clear from the comfort of their clubhouse.

The Royal & Ancient Clubhouse is the temple of golf, the game (more a way of life to many) which St Andrews claims to have created in its present form, supported by a document dating back to 1552. This deed, bearing the seal of Archbishop Hamilton, refers to the public ownership of the Links, which golfers shared with shooting, football and grazing livestock. 'Noblemen and Gentlemen' formed themselves into a society of golfers in 1766, and in 1834 King William IV became the society's patron, conferring on it the title 'The Royal and Ancient Golf Club of St Andrews.' Since then, millions of golf balls have been driven (and some lost) over these acres of green sward which Americans especially treat with veneration.

The Royal & Ancient Clubhouse at evening, when the word round takes on a different meaning at the bar. Behind, under its distinctive illuminated dome, is the former Hamilton Hall of Residence of the University of St Andrews. It was made over at a cost of millions and renamed Hamilton Grand. Golfers sleep in its luxurious apartments before the thrill of the Old Course in the morning - weather permitting.

Who more fitting to dominate the fascinating exhibits in the British Golf Museum in St Andrews than Old Tom Morris in bronze, with his earlier self behind? Born in North Street, St Andrews in 1821, he was on the Links at the age of six with a golf club. As the winner of four Open Championships, and since he laid out the Old Course in its present form, the 18th hole is fittingly named after him. Golf must have been in the Morris genes, since his son, Young Tom, won the Open Championship Belt before the age of 21. Golfing pilgrims can find the funerary monuments of father and son in the Cathedral's cemetery.

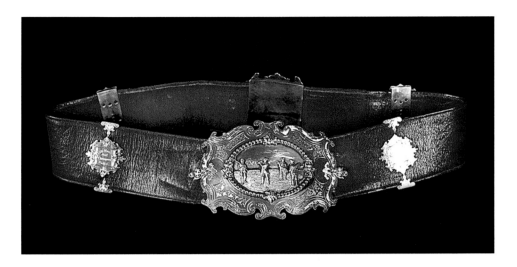

(Top): After his third consecutive Open Championship win Young Tom Morris was allowed to keep this belt. His 'challenging relationship' with his father is the theme of the feature film Tommy's Honour. Jack Lowden (right) plays Young Tom, and (left), Theresa Bradley, treading the red carpet to the premiere in St Andrews, is Young Tom's glamorous mother.

Bishop Henry Wardlaw gives his blessing to St Mary's College, which survived the sledgehammers of the Reformation. This wonderful statue by David Annand was unveiled in 2013, near where the first college building (St John's College) and Wardlaw's pedagogy are known to have existed. The new statue is modelled on the surviving remains of Bishop Wardlaw's effigy, held in the Cathedral Museum, the effigy's head having been found hidden in the Cathedral's perimeter wall, its torso having been put to purpose as a window lintel on South Street, and its accompanying plaque having been discovered as a South Street paving stone in the nineteenth century.

34

(Left): Bishop Henry Wardlaw, founder of the University, presides over students dining in St Salvator's Hall.

(Right): Bishop James Kennedy, founder of St Salvator's College, is also a presence in St Salvator Hall's dining room. He carries his precious creation, an offering to the Almighty for His blessing.

St Salvator's Quadrangle, formerly the site of St Salvator's College, founded and generously endowed by Bishop James Kennedy in 1450. The Chapel on the right was founded in the same year, and served for several centuries as a parish church as well as the University's chapel. Students and staff continue to worship in the Chapel, though female students have discarded the mortar boards that were once a part of Chapel dress. The teaching blocks are nineteenth century replacements.

In the magnificent interior of St Salvator's Chapel Dr Tom Wilkinson, the University's brilliant organist and conductor of the acclaimed Chapel Choir, accompanies a student to an appreciative audience of one. At the Sunday morning service these pews are occupied by students, alumni, and University staff.

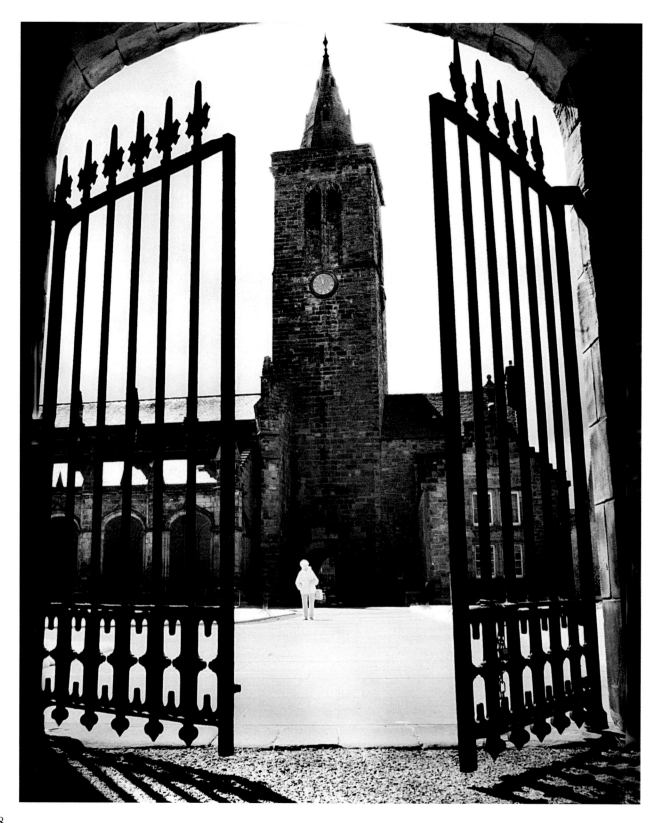

St Leonard's Chapel, built in the sixteenth century, has an exceptional atmosphere of peace and piety, perhaps because it stands on the site of a medieval hospice established by Culdee monks. Having fallen into ruin in the eighteenth century, it was restored in the twentieth century through the Russell Trust, founded by Sir David Russell in memory of his son Pat, killed in action in Italy in 1944. The Pilgrim Trust also contributed to the Chapel's sympathetic restoration. Here students gather once weekly in term time for Compline, with the Chapel's own choir in the service of thanksgiving at the close of day, presided over by various members of the University's dedicated Chaplaincy team.

Two students confer under the illuminated tower of St Salvator's Chapel, with lunar light adding to the atmosphere.

In the serenity of the grounds of St Mary's College students like to congregate on the lawns in the summer term sun to eat lunch and discuss what they will do in the long vacation. The old archway, relocated to St Mary's College grounds well over a century ago, is a backdrop for a discussion on studies - or perhaps for planning a party with friends.

(Over page): St Mary's College, part of Scotland's architectural heritage. On this site had previously stood the medieval College of St John; it was replaced in 1538 by St Mary's College, which survived the wreckage of the Reformation.

41

Bicycles are the preferred locomotive power of the students of St Andrews.

The Roundel stands on the corner of South Street, its front block dated to the sixteenth century, but the regular five-bay windows suggest the late seventeenth century. The house's east gable displays the Haldenstone arms. James Haldenstone became Prior of St Andrews in 1417, and Dean of Theology in the new University of St Andrews. He was noted as an inquisitor of heretics.

Exclusively for women who were at last admitted to the University of St Andrews in 1892, University Hall was opened in 1896, the first female university residence in Scotland. It was loved by its residents, who planted potatoes in the surrounding ground in the First World War; they formed life-long friendships as they huddled round coal fires with cocoa mugs and toasting forks. The Wardlaw Wing with its tower was added in 1912. The Hall became a mixed residence in 1994.

The University of St Andrews has been blessed with generous benefactors. Edward Stephen Harkness, Scottish-American friend of Principal James Irvine, gave his support 'to the project of a collegiate revival in the oldest university of his forebears' homeland' (Ronald Cant, the University's historian). Harkness gave £100,000, most of which was to go towards the building of a hall of residence for men students. The first section of St Salvator's Hall was opened in 1930 and the complete building (accommodating 130 students) in 1940. It now accommodates women also. Its reputation was enhanced when Prince William chose to live in the Hall for part of his time at the University from 2001-5.

The Bute Building within St Mary's College grounds, made possible by the munificence of the 3rd Marquis of Bute, elected Rector of the University in 1892 and re-elected in 1895. In the 1890s he rebuilt some of the Priory building; it is believed that he hoped to see the entire Cathedral rebuilt.

This doocot in the grounds of St Mary's College was built in 1789 to replace an earlier round one. Known as a Lectern doocot, the surviving one was erected to house white birds only, with the janitors given the authority to preserve pristine purity by wringing the necks of cross-bred birds. The culled product of the pigeon house was for the Principal's plate only. There have been no white doves for years, a loss to the appeal of the enclosed policies.

An unusual perspective of the University Library, built in the 1970s to accommodate an increasing number of students. Here the laptop is mightier than the pen, as students' assignments are delivered electronically to their lecturers.

The building on North Street which houses Anthropology, the essential study of our species in peace and discord.

Erected between 1923 and 1929, the Younger Graduation Hall on North Street was a magnificent gift by Dr and Mrs James Younger of Mount Melville. The opening ceremony was performed by the late Queen Elizabeth the Queen Mother when Duchess of York. The Hall, on which no expense seems to have been spared, with its marble-clad staircase and sprung floor, is claimed to be the finest dance floor in Scotland. For several generations it has echoed to the proud applause of parents as their children go up to receive their well-earned degrees.

The Whyte-Melville Memorial Fountain in cobbled Market Street, St Andrews, erected by Lady Catherine Melville in 1880, in memory of her son George Whyte Melville, the Victorian novelist and horseman who was born in St Andrews and who was killed in a riding accident in 1878. His profile is on the fountain. Water is arching again from the fountain after a long stoppage, support for the resumption of the flow coming from the St Andrews Common Good Fund as well as other sources. The fountain has become a filling station for seagulls.

The Sports Centre's changing room facilities on Hepburn Gardens show that good architectural character is not found only in the oldest parts of St Andrews.

The Physics Building on the North Haugh, the green acreage on the western approach to St Andrews developed by the University from the 1960s onward, after an earlier scheme to erect science buildings in the centre of the town had been rejected.

Science at the University of St Andrews

'The teaching of Science has a long history at St Andrews University, stretching back to the Scottish Enlightenment. Today the University is very strong in the Sciences, admitting as many Science as Arts students. The Science Faculty consists of eight Schools (Biology; Chemistry; Computer Science; Geography and Sustainable Development; Earth and Environmental Sciences; Mathematics; Physics and Astronomy; Psychology and Neuroscience), and most of these Schools have their buildings and laboratories on the North Haugh.'

Professor David O'Hagan, Head of School of Chemistry.

An image showing many faces of a student, paying tribute to Sir David Brewster, inventor of the kaleidoscope. Principal of the United College of the University from 1838-59, he is acknowledged worldwide as the founding father of modern optics.

Chemistry at the University of St Andrews

'Chemistry has been taught at St Andrews since 1811. In the early twentieth century chemists at St Andrews carried out important research into carbohydrate (sugar) chemistry establishing the structures of some of the basic sugars of biology. In more recent years the School of Chemistry has established itself as a leading one in the UK where interdisciplinary chemistry is a feature. It has developed a very strong interface with biochemistry and medicine and there are important overlaps with Physics through advanced materials research. Modern state of the art teaching laboratories are located in the Medical and Biological Science Building, and the School of Chemistry is graduating its largest undergraduate classes in its 200 year history.'

Professor David O' Hagan, Head of School of Chemistry

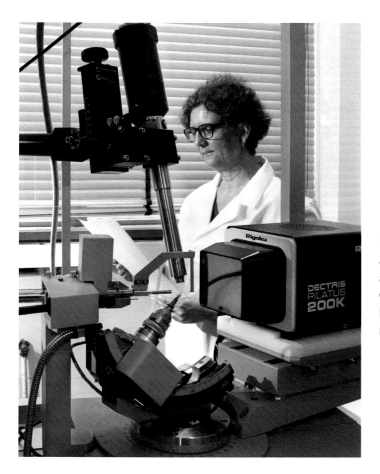

Professor Alexandra M Z Slawin made history as the first female Professor of Chemistry at the University when she was awarded a Chair in 2004. This dedicated crystallographer has published over 1000 research papers, reporting the structures of new molecules.

(Top): Undergraduates in the chemistry laboratory racing each other to purify their samples.

(Bottom): An undergraduate examines the sample he has prepared, after removing solvent on a rotary evaporator.

Research chemist Dr Federico Grillo analyses a sample, using a large X-Ray photoelectron spectroscopy instrument. The machine operates under very high vacuum and needs to be reinforced with steel to withstand being crushed by atmospheric pressure.

Physics at the University of St Andrews

'Since the mid-1960s the J.F. Allen building has been home to St Andrews' internationally renowned physics research. Before this time, the University's physics research labs were located on the Scores in Edgecliffe House, where one of the UK's first lasers was built in a converted bedroom, and liquid hydrogen and helium were produced and studied in the shed at the back. The technologies that grew from these modest beginnings now underpin today's world-leading physics research in St Andrews. Helium now liquefied in-house on an industrial scale, cools the superconducting magnets used to study designer quantum materials. Advanced lasers track the movement of electrons through a solar cell with a trillionth of a second precision, and image and manipulate individual biological cells for medical diagnosis and treatment. Today's laboratories include advanced clean-rooms for semiconductor processing, high-precision crystal growth facilities, and ultra-low vibration laboratories that house specialised microscopes that can see the individual atoms on the surface of a solid.'

Professor Graham Turnbull, School of Physics and Astronomy.

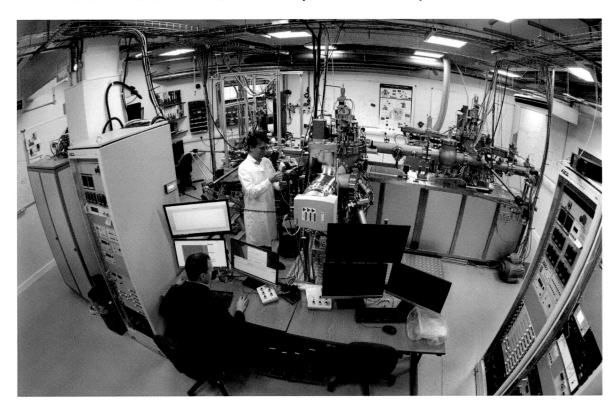

At the Centre for Designer Quantum Materials in the School of Physics and Astronomy sophisticated apparatus is used with ease by Dr Peter Wahl (standing). The machines shown allow scientists to build new materials, a single atom layer at a time, enabling the construction of entirely new compounds which do not naturally exist, and which have specially tailored physical properties.

A molecular-beam epitaxy machine is operated in the Centre for Designer Materials at the School of Physics and Astronomy by Dr Philip King. Inside the stainless steel chamber conditions of extremely high vacuum (similar to those found in outer space) and high temperatures allow the creation of new materials which are only a single atomic layer in thickness.

Biology at the University of St. Andrews

'Biology originated from the merger of several separate departments: Botany, Zoology, Physiology and Pharmacology, and Anatomy and Experimental Pathology and Biochemistry. Much of the teaching and administration took place in the Bute Building, a happy arrangement which lasted until 2010, when much of Biology teaching was moved to its present locations at the North Haugh.'
Professor Jim Naismith, Chemical Biology.

Dr Clarissa Melo Czekster is intent on her research. As part of the Bioenergetics module, Year 3 Biology students attend a workshop on the use of the Seahorse apparatus. Students analyse Seahorse data and quiz researchers at St Andrews on their use of this technology. This novel technology is being developed to assess mitochondrial function to enable the prediction of disease progression and the response to treatment.

Lights burn late at the Biomedical Sciences Research Complex, searching for solutions which will benefit us all.

Medicine at the University of St Andrews

'Medicine has been taught at St Andrews for many, many years. In the recent past the School of Medicine has taught a BSc in Medicine which contributes towards two years of a five years' medical training programme. Students complete their studies at the 4 other Scottish Medical Schools or at Medical Schools in Manchester and London. Teaching is to a very high standard and now has a large clinical element including clinical examination and communication skills. From 2018 St Andrews will also teach medicine through a graduate entry scheme (run jointly with the University of Dundee). Students will graduate with a joint degree from both universities.'

Professor David Crossman, Dean of Medicine.

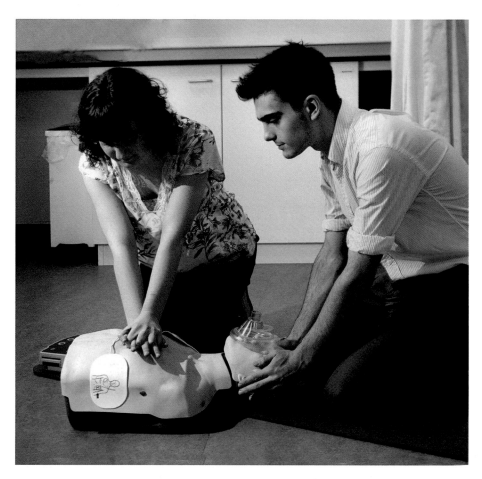

The University of St Andrews has an international reputation for the quality of its medical training, and the care, professional and personal, it bestows on its students. Here a technique which could help us to survive a heart attack is practised, performed to current guidelines, using external cardiac compression to maintain cardiac output following cardiac arrest.

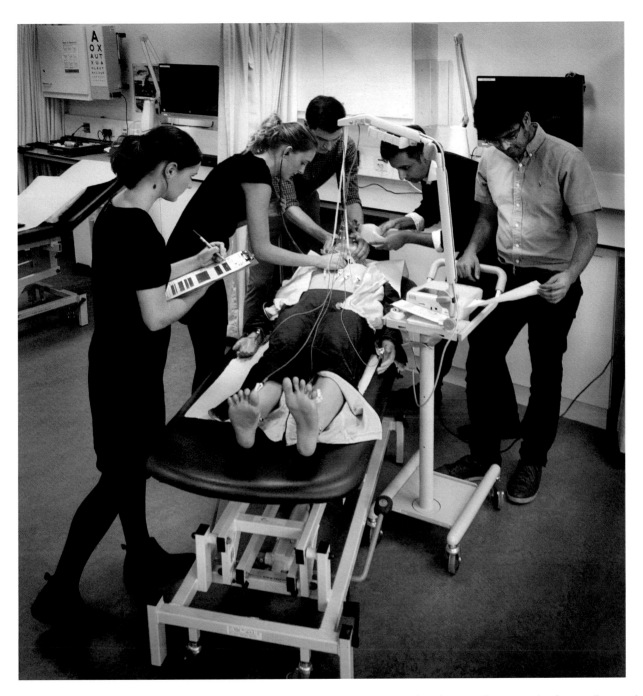

Doctors of the future at the University practise emergency evaluation and support of a collapsed patient, using well-developed models that can respond to different interactions. Second and third year medical students mentor and tutor younger medical students, mostly through practical workshops, demonstrations and mock examinations.

Marine Mammal Science
at the University of St Andrews

'The Sea Mammal Research Unit (SMRU) is at the forefront of marine mammal research all over the world. These species spend large parts of their lives hidden beneath the water, so SMRU researchers have developed methods to study these elusive animals, finding out where they go, what they do and the effect that human activities have on them.'

Dr Phil Irving, Science Manager

Three bottlenose dolphins jumping out of the sea, off the Scottish coast. (photo credit: M. Arso; SMRU).

Harbour seal with SMRU GPS phone tag. The tags allow researchers to find out where seals go and where they feed over several months in the wild. (photo credit: M. Arso; SMRU)

Harbour seals are counted on land using three different cameras mounted on a helicopter. A thermal imager is essential for locating seals on shore, a video camera with laser rangefinder helps to determine the precise location of the group and a high-resolution digital camera is used to differentiate between species. (photo credit: C. Morris; SMRU).

On a visit to St Andrews in the summer of 1982, Her Majesty the Queen was presented with a replica of the famous red gown to hand over to her grandson William. It must have inspired the Prince, because he decided to study at St Andrews.

Arise, Prince William, M.A. In the summer of 2005 the future king graduated from the University of St Andrews, capped by the late Sir Kenneth Dover, then Chancellor of the University, with Jim Douglas the bedellus holding the hood.

A proud grandmother congratulates her grandson on graduating in 2005 while Dr Brian Lang, the then Principal and Vice-Chancellor of the University of St Andrews looks on.

Two future kings, father and son, and Prince Charles's wife, Camilla, Duchess of Cornwall, at Prince William's graduation ceremony.

Professor Sally Mapstone, the new Principal and Vice-Chancellor of the University of St Andrews, walks in procession beside the Chancellor, Menzies Campbell, Baron Campbell of Pittenweem in June 2017.

The historical array of the Maces of the University of St Andrews, proudly carried in ceremonials. These creations by master craftsmen range from the medieval to the modern. Their bearers are immaculately attired.

Rain does not spoil Graduation Day, when lecturers and professors turn out in their colours to applaud their students and meet the proud parents.

The colours of academic success are paraded round St Salvator's Quadrangle on a day to remember with pride.

A symbolic globe of future possibilities is hoisted on Graduation Day. Students from the University of St Andrews pursue careers and success all over the world.

(Top): Clocks, like people, become exhausted with the passage of time. The St. Salvator's ones were fortunate in finding a patron in local philanthropist Mrs Cookie Matheson who paid for new clocks.

(Bottom): Archbishop Desmond Tutu, the South African peacemaker, was a most welcome visitor to the University. He was made patron of the University's Centre for the Study of Religion and Politics in 2005.

(Clockwise from top): Neil Oliver, on-screen archaeologist and coastal wanderer, signs a copy of his novel *Master of Shadows* at St Andrews. The controversial Oxford evolutionary biologist Richard Dawkins came to St Andrews in 2015 to launch his autobiography about his life in science, *Brief Candle in the Dark*. Michael Douglas, star of the screen, received an honorary degree in 2006, accompanied by his actress wife Catherine Zeta-Jones.

(Top): The actress Joanna Lumley clearly thought it was 'Absolutely Fabulous' to receive an honorary degree from the University of St Andrews in 2006. Is the University's Chancellor Lord Campbell of Pittenweem rehearsing a political speech under her expert tutelage?

(Bottom): Two gentlemen who believe in the elixir of laughter: the comedy writer the late Frank Muir, Rector of the University of St Andrews 1977-1979, and the Dalai Lama, exiled spiritual leader of the Tibetan people, who received an honorary degree in 1993.

(Clockwise from top left): Sir Nicholas Parsons, Rector of the University, 1988-91. Helen Mirren, Hon. D.Litt.,1999. J.K. Rowling, Hon. D.Litt., 2000.

(Clockwise from top left) :Michael Palin of 'Monty Python' fame, Hon. D.Litt., 2017. John Cleese, Hon.D.Litt.,1971. Terry Jones, scholar of mediaeval history and literature, Hon. D.Litt., 2013. When the comedian John Cleese was made Rector of the University of St Andrews in 1970, he described himself as the first 'silly Rector' in the University's history, but refrained from any Basil Fawlty antics, to the disappointment of his audience.

(Clockwise from top left): The reclusive Bob Dylan, poetic songwriter, singer, Nobel Prize Laureate, graced the University of St Andrews in 2004 with his presence to receive an honorary degree, though he did not bring his guitar. George Bush, former United States President and golfing enthusiast, visited the Royal & Ancient in 1994 during the Autumn Meeting. Former American Secretary of State Hillary Clinton received an honorary degree at St Andrews in 2013. Noam Chomsky, linguist and philosopher, honorary graduate, St Andrews, in 2012, (left), with Stephen Reicher, Wardlaw Professor of Psychology and Neuroscience, St Andrews.

Saint Andrew, depicted by a student in the Kate Kennedy Procession, carries his unique iconic cross, the revered symbol of Scotland. Come late spring, historical figures, saints and assassins, appear on the streets of St Andrews in the Kate Kennedy Club Procession. The Club derives its name from Kate, niece of Bishop James Kennedy, Bishop-Chancellor of the University, founder of St Salvator's College and an outstanding academic statesman.

Kate and her uncle, Bishop Kennedy, revisit St Andrews. Those who insist that the Kate Kennedy Procession is a continuation of a medieval pageant are directed to the writings of the late Dr Ronald Cant, the University's historian, who states: "it would seem to have originated in 1849 as an end-of-the-season 'rag' of the final year students in Arts." However old, the Procession attracts many onlookers, with female students now permitted to participate, instead of being 'represented' by male students in female costumes.

Andrew Bell, citizen of St Andrews, matriculated at the United College in 1769. Well known as the creator of the Madras system of education, both Madras College, St Andrews, and Bell Baxter School, Cupar, were founded from the wealth he accumulated over his lifetime. In 1819 this pious philanthropist was made a Canon of Westminster Abbey.

Murder and mayhem on the peaceful streets of St Andrews as three students re-enact the assassination of Archbishop James Sharp at the beginning of the Kate Kennedy Procession. The Primate of Scotland was dragged from his carriage on the outskirts of St Andrews on 3rd May 1679.

Four Marys in fetching gowns and stylish headgear line up for the Kate Kennedy Procession, recalling the ballad:

> Last night there were four Marys;
> Tonight there'll be but three:
> There was Mary Beaton and Mary Seaton
> And Mary Carmichael and me.

Sport at the University of St Andrews

'The University continues to invest in making sports central to the student experience, and in January 2015 embarked on a major £14m redevelopment and extension of the Sports Centre. The new indoor facilities now feature an 8-court sports arena, a 110-station gym and a dedicated strength and conditioning suite for our performance athletes. The original dance studio has also been refurbished and a new technical climbing wall has been installed in the 4-court sports hall. The construction of a 4-court indoor tennis centre adjacent to the Sports Centre is due to be completed in December 2017. This will cement a major, seven-year investment in sport at St Andrews and bring our indoor facilities in line with the rest of the estate.'

Fergus Knight, Marketing & Business Development Manager at the University of St Andrews.

Enthusiastic Team Captains of the University's Athletics Union. The AU is the umbrella organisation for the support and development of sport and sports clubs at the University, run by students, for students. It provides structure and advice to over sixty clubs and several thousand members.

The grass pitches at University Park are renowned across the country for being among the finest in Scotland and have been praised by many professionals who have visited St Andrews, including FC Barcelona, Manchester United FC and Scottish Rugby. Dundee United Football Club have based their training ground at University Park since 2009 and continue to receive support from the Strength and Conditioning Team for both their first team and development squads. Here they do the hard work that gets goals.

The iconic scene of the mass run across the West Sands in the acclaimed film 'Chariots of Fire' is repeated by enthusiasts. What they lack in puff is made up for in dedication.

The red gown is an essential item of apparel for the student arriving in St Andrews for the first time. It is fashionable, and given the cold of the east coast, can be wrapped around for warmth. Introduced to Scotland from the continent in the 1600's, they were being worn at St Andrews seventy or so years later.

Gentlemen, if you run out of shaving foam on Raisin Monday, forget it, because there won't be a canister left in the town. Shaving foam is the main ammunition for the battle between students, now on Lower College Lawn. Raisin Weekend is based on the tradition of 'academic' families at the University. Third or fourth year students volunteer to act as 'parents' to interested first year students, introducing their 'children' to academic and social life at St Andrews . First year students traditionally presented their parents with a bottle of wine (formerly a pound of raisins) for which they received a receipt written in Latin. As for the layer of shaving foam on the lawn on Raisin Monday, it disappears when the grass is 'shaved.'

Each year on 30 April torches are lit on St Andrews pier for the Gaudie, a procession led by pipers. The history books offer no enlightenment as to the origins of this tradition, but it is believed to commemorate the heroism of a former student, John Honey, who swam out to rescue crew members on the ship the Janet of Macduff, which was sinking off the East Sands. As a result of injuries sustained from a fallen mast on his final swim to shore, having rescued men, Honey later died. The Gaudie students observe a minute's silence, and a wreath is thrown off the pier while a traditional University song, the 'Gaudeamus,' is sung.

Some students may find it difficult to rise for lectures, but a considerable number of them were up before dawn on the first day of May in order to participate in the traditional May Dip. How long they lasted in the bracing North Sea is another matter.

The harmonious choir of St Salvator's Chapel take to the street to sing. Members are eligible for a choral scholarship, which includes subsidised singing lessons, free participation in the choir's annual tour, when they enchant various venues in Europe. Another welcome perk of the choral scholarship is Sunday lunch.

St Andrews students and citizens like to sing, from sacred music to operas, and Gilbert and Sullivan's collaborations are favourites for staging. Utopia, Limited, or The Flowers of Progress, was the penultimate collaboration of the composer and librettist of genius, premiering on 7 October 1893 for a run of 245 performances. It did not achieve the success of most of their earlier productions. The opera, rarely performed since then, is a satire in which a kingdom in the South Seas copies every aspect of British life, but, as it turns out, with too much enthusiasm for its own good. Peter Sutton played the part of King Paramount with aplomb, and Alice Gold was in convincing voice as Lady Sophy the English governess.

The Modern Schoolgirl

The modern schoolgirl - and boy - have a backpack instead of a barrow, as depicted in this humorous illustration by Cynicus (Martin Anderson, educated at Madras College). Nowadays she learns about her own identity and how to conduct her life from an ipad, not a tome. St Andrews has several schools: Canongate Primary; Lawhead Primary; Greyfriars Roman Catholic Primary; Madras College; and the private co-educational boarding and day St Leonards School. All are schools of quality and care, dedicated staff providing a wide education to their charges. Greyfriars is not restricted to pupils of the Roman Catholic faith.

The cloisters of Madras College, which, after much public debate, is to be replaced by a modern school, though not on the same site. Let us hope that the fine old building off South Street has a secure future through a new use.

The light fantastic: Madras College pupils are mesmerized by the refraction of light, when it bends as it passes at a slant through an interface between two materials, a phenomenon familiar to fishermen, who see their fishing lines appear to bend in the water. This set-up shows how light refracts when it enters our eyes, and how an image is created on the back of our retinas.

Bulb growing competition at Lawhead Primary School through the Edina Trust. The children have had to record, online, the progress of the bulbs since planting them in the Autumn.

And put a pencil in my hand,
A copy book at my command;
And let my final effort be
To ring a rhyme of homely glee.
        Robert W. Service.

There is plenty of glee among the pupils of Canongate Primary School, built in 1972 in extensive grounds beside the inspirational Botanic Garden.

The joy of books at Greyfriars Roman Catholic School, established in 1959, but not fully funded until taken over by the County Council in 1969. At that time it was relocated to the old Burgh School, and in August 2007 it moved to newly refurbished accommodation at Kilrymont Road.

A Clipper butterfly (*Parthenos sylvia*), found in South and South-East Asia, mostly in forested areas, spreads its gorgeous wings in the Butterfly House in the Botanic Garden, an essential place to visit to experience in close proximity the colourful but fragile wonder of nature.

The original Botanic Garden was in the grounds of St Mary's College, and the present one was created from two fields in the early 1960s. The property of the University, the Garden was leased to North East Fife District Council, now Fife Council, which has been responsible for its management ever since. The Garden, which could not function without its dedicated volunteers, is now administered by the St Andrews Botanic Garden Trust. It has become an increasingly popular site for public entertainment such as concerts and opera, generating valuable income. *Betula pendula*, commonly known as silver birch, makes an appealing reflection.

New Zealand flax, *Phormium tenax*, in its glory in the Botanic Garden. About 8000 species of ferns, herbaceous plants, shrubs and trees are grown in the Garden. Some are native to Scotland but most grow wild in other regions of the world. All those outdoors are hardy and can be cultivated successfully in the climate around St Andrews.

Street dancers The Ruggets demonstrate their amazing acrobatics at the opening of the 'Byre in the Botanics' 2017 season, offering varieties of artistic shows. The troupe has performed with big stars such as Justin Bieber and Rita Ora.

The medieval Priory required power to turn its water wheels, so a 'lade,' or channel was cut to bring water from the Kinness Burn. The Reformation didn't stop the flow, though the wheels it served were probably wantonly wrecked. St Andrews needed meal, so the lade turned out the town's daily bread. Around 1860 the channel was filled in. The Victorians with their seeds and spades began planting round the lade, creating the sylvan and floral Lade Braes walk, a most peaceful place to perambulate, or rest and read.

I wander on the Lade Braes, where I used to walk with you,
And purple are the woods of Mount Melville, budding new,
But I cannot bear to look, for the tears keep coming so,
And the Spring has lost the freshness which it had a year ago.

Yet often I could fancy, where the pathway takes a turn,
I shall see you in a moment, coming round beside the burn,
Coming round beside the burn, with your swinging step and free,
And your face lit up with pleasure at the sudden sight of me.
                                        R.F. Murray.

(Over page): This heart-warming coastal meadow of poppies on the bank of the Kinness Burn by the East Sands has been created by local school pupils as part of the St Andrews Biodiversity Challenge, delivered by Keep Scotland Beautiful. This tranquil area will help to support biodiversity, providing a valuable habitat for pollinators and other wildlife, whilst bringing colour and interest.

113

115

Horsemen and carriages containing haughty ladies used to trot and roll through the West Port, the main approach to the city, in past times of peace and turbulence. Stone from the earlier gate was recycled when the West Port was erected in 1589 by a local mason, using Edinburgh's Netherbow Port as a model. Cars may enter, but at a slow speed.

How many people remember travelling across this viaduct at the back entrance to the Botanic Garden? It qualifies as a historic monument, part of the track of the independent St Andrews Railway Company, founded in 1851 to build a branch line from the University town to the nearby mainline railway. The line opened in 1852, and was sold to the North British Railway in 1877. When the Tay Road Bridge opened in 1966, 40% of the line's passenger earnings were lost immediately. Decline continued and the line closed completely in 1969.

The spire of Holy Trinity Church, with the two antique lamp standards outside the Burgh Chambers bearing the assertion: 'While I breathe, I hope.'

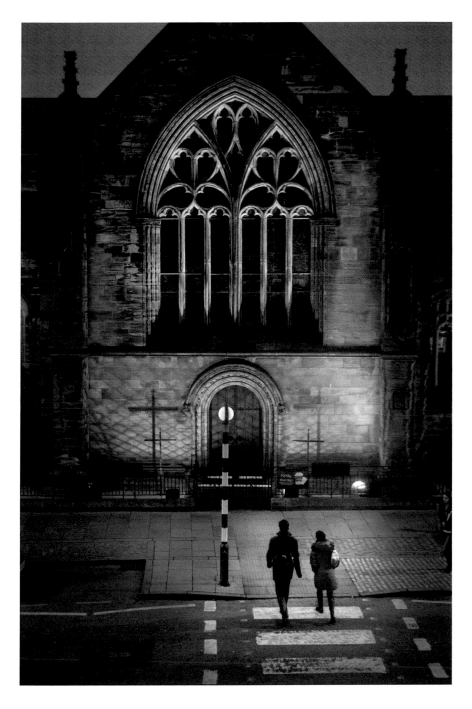

Established in the twelfth century, the massive Holy Trinity's peace was broken when John Knox, arch-enemy of Catholicism, leaned out of the pulpit, his fiery sermon sending the wreckers to the Cathedral at the violent start of the Scottish Reformation. Today, however, the sermons are welcoming and conciliatory. Holy Trinity has been twice remodelled, by Robert Balfour in 1798-1800, and in 1907-09 by P. MacGregor Chalmers. The stained glass by Douglas Strachan and others is exquisite.

The 'Good Physician' window in Holy Trinity Church, depicting the invitation of Christ (centre): 'Come unto Me all that labour and are heavy laden and I will give you rest.' (Left), Saint Luke, the beloved physician, carries his gospel scroll, while (right), Saint Andrew, the first apostle, bears witness. This beautiful window was created around 1890 by Alexander Ballantine and his son James. Alexander was a glass stainer and house painter who also made traditional windows, but found his true gift in stained glass.

120

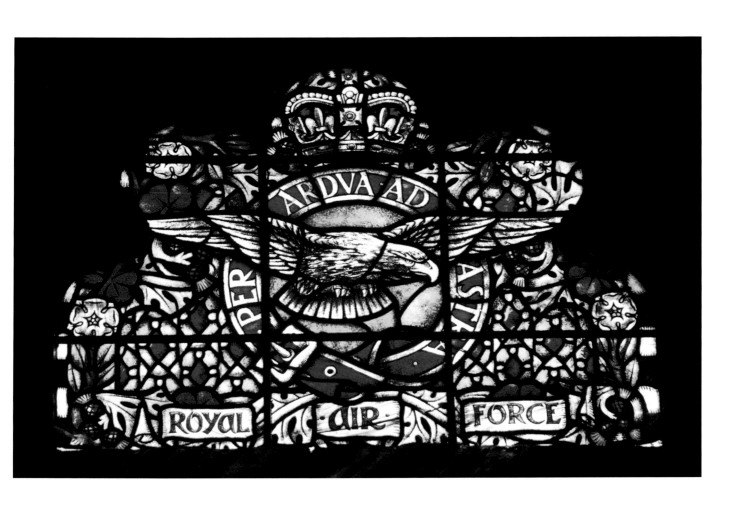

The badge of the Royal Air Force is reproduced in a memorial window in the Clerestory of Holy Trinity Church. The other sixteen windows show the badges of our defenders on land and sea.

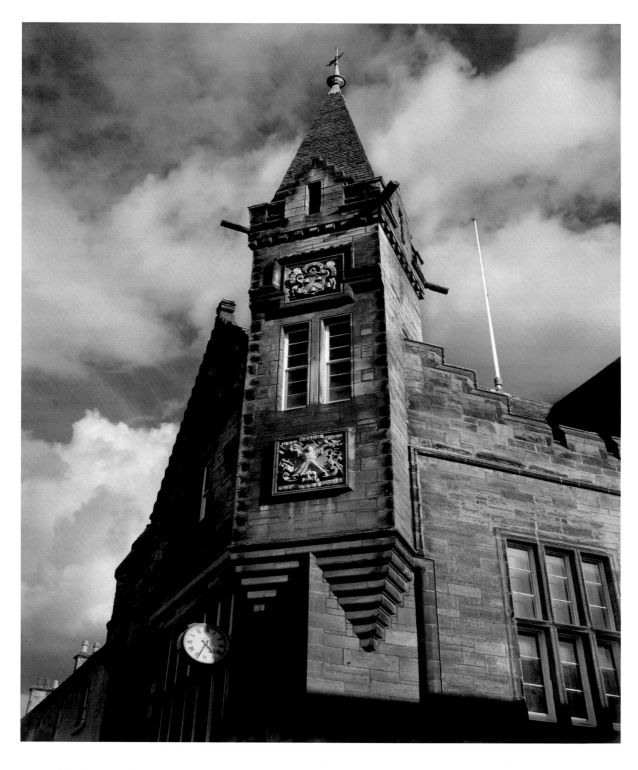

The Burgh Chambers of St Andrews, 1858-62, by J. Anderson Hamilton, 'suppressing some of his usual exuberance. Baronial with a Flemish flavour.'

John Gifford, *The Buildings of Scotland: Fife*, 1988.

South Court leads to the Byre Theatre which opened its doors in an old byre in the Abbey Street dairy farm in 1933, thanks to the vision and perseverance of local journalist and playwright Alexander B. Paterson. Too small to contain the laughter and, sometimes, tears of the rapt audiences, the theatre was demolished in 1969. Now St Andrews has a magnificent new theatre of stone and glass, run by the University.

The lion with the manicured mane on top of the fountain close to the Royal & Ancient Clubhouse is an elegant pun. Designed by the outstanding Fife architect Sir Robert Lorimer, it was erected by Sir Hugh Lyon Playfair's children in fond memory of their outstanding father, Provost of St Andrews and photographic pioneer. A small fountain at the bottom serves thirsty dogs.

Hope Park & Martyrs Church of Scotland, St Mary's Place, was designed and built by the distinguished architects Peddie & Kinnear in 1864-65, with the hall added by Gillespie & Scott. At time of writing this welcoming place of worship offers light lunches on Tuesdays and Thursdays.

Mrs Annette Harmar, wealthy widow of a distiller, migrated from London to St Andrews, and donated the majority of her fortune to financing the construction of the new Catholic Church of St James, consecrated in 1910. The resident congregation is swelled by visitors, and by the substantial number of international students who are members of the University's Catholic Society, and who have the use of Mrs Harmar's house through the generosity of the Stevens family and the Archdiocese.

The impressive Jacobean façade of Gibson House (built 1880-82) on Argyll Street, a care home where citizens of St Andrews live out their twilight years in comfort and companionship.

A late Georgian tenement given Tudor details in the 1920s, it was the former home of the St Andrews Citizen Newspaper, and is now the spacious premises of J & G Innes, Stationers, Booksellers, Art Supplies & Gift Shop, with gallery space available above.

This bell in the car park beside the Students' Union on St Mary's Place goes unnoticed, but once rang out to summon the pupils of the West Infants Primary School to their desks, with slates to do their sums on, and, if they were naughty, a tawse to make their small palms smart.

(Over page): Craigtoun Park, former estate of the Youngers. The Dutch Village is a popular recreational place for all ages and all-comers.

In 1929 John Morris who ran a local plumber's business at 126 Market Street purchased derelict property at 115, 117 and 119 North Street. The New Picture House opened for business in December 1930, showing a popular musical of the day 'No no Nanette.' The cinema had seating for 950 and was in direct competition with The Cinema House which was also situated in North Street. As times changed there was only enough business for one cinema in town and The Cinema House closed in 1981. So what's showing tonight at the New? Rascals Bar adjacent to the cinema serves award-winning food, burgers a speciality.

This splendid specimen of a Highland cow is part of the Strathtyrum fold on the outskirts of St Andrews. Balgove Larder opened in September 2010, following a complete and sympathetic rebuild of the derelict farm steading that had previously been used to store cattle, grain and farm machinery at different times. A spokesperson for the Larder says proudly: 'Conceived from a love of fresh, Scottish produce, Balgove has become a hub for top notch locally reared, grown, stalked, caught, handmade, and prepared foods. Scotland is home to the world's best beef, game, seafood and produce. Instead of seeing this amazing food shipped off to the far corners of the globe, our desire is to keep it right here on home turf.'

On the streets of St Andrews folks carry cardboard boxes bearing the name of Fisher & Donaldson as if they contain precious relics and not sponges. Located on Church Street, the emporium of the palate is a fifth generation business owned and operated by the Milne family since 1919. Be patient in the queue: the personable ladies in their boaters won't run out of fudge-filled doughnuts.

St Andrews, home of golf, is also the home of gelato. Along towards the Cathedral end of South Street is Jannettas, with constant queues in fair weather. This ultra-successful business was started over a century ago by Bennett Jannetta, who emigrated from Italy. He was the great-grandfather of the current co-owner Nicola Hazel, who has been running the business with her husband Owen for over 21 years. Jannettas still use the recipe that brings them fame far beyond Fife, making their gelato on the original site, using traditional artisan machinery.

One of the oldest pubs in St Andrews, the Keys Bar on Market Street is in a building dating to the mid nineteenth century, when men swilled beer from tankards and smoked clay pipes. It is possible that an earlier hostelry occupied the site, in which case the Reformation wreckers may have slaked their throats, parched from the dust of the Cathedral statues which they had helped to demolish. The Society of St Andrews Golfers used to eat and imbibe in the Keys. It boasts that it stocks 270 different whiskies. Why doesn't someone tell the wee fellow that he's underage?

Mica, aka the do-it-yourself store in St Andrews, founded and run with super efficiency and friendliness by the Hood family dynasty and assistants, who can lead you, among thousands of items, to what you want in seconds.

Someone should make a song about the extended family of 16 meerkats living together in St Andrews Aquarium, delighting all who have the pleasure of meeting them, including the many schoolchildren who visit the Aquarium. His name is Dipper, son of Catherine and William, and he's on the lookout for his lunch.

His official name is Black Pacu, his pet name Bonzo. When his doting owner died, his daughter asked the Aquarium in St Andrews to give him a home. He is a member of the piranha family, but your fingers are safe. He is a citizen of the Amazon, but is now a naturalized Scot, most happy in his spacious tank with the orange Tiger Oscar, also from the Amazon.

Yup-yup, a Chinese water dragon, seems to be doing a dance for spectators in the Aquarium. Where does his cute name come from? His keeper and friend Cara Anderson reveals: 'My colleague and I both watched the TV show Sesame Street as children and one of the puppets were these aliens that could only say "yup yup yup yup". When the Chinese water dragons first arrived, from a breeder down south, they were just a few months old, with these giant eyes far too big for their heads, making them look like the alien characters from Sesame Street. He's a friendly wee chap, and I hand-feed him his crickets and locusts. He still has a fair bit of growing to do as they can reach three feet from nose to tail.'

The pun is on the word Pole, because that was the nationality of the wielder of clippers and scissors therein and because the red and white of a barber's pole are also the Polish national colours. Training as a hairdresser in his native Krakow when war broke out in 1939, Michael Zamora was conscripted into the army. Michael came to Scotland when General Sikorski was reforming the Polish Army. He took over the hairdressers shop at 134 South Street in the 1960s, retiring in 1995. The shop is still called The Barber's Pole in tribute and respect to a likeable man with a story to tell his customers. Michael is seen in the photograph standing beside Winston Churchill at Leuchars Station during a visit by Churchill to General Sikorski in St Andrews in October 1940. Who knows but he offered to give our wartime leader a trim in the waiting room before the arrival of his train?

Farmore Interiors on South Street offer furnishings for the discerning.

The bridal boutique Enchanted at the corner of South Street and Abbey Street deals in irresistible dreams.

The name Auchterlonie is synonymous with golf equipment. Laurie Auchterlonie, son of Willie, the Open winner of 1893, was born in 1904, and probably played with a club instead of a rattle in his crib. Like his father, he was appointed honorary professional of the Royal & Ancient, and, using his knowledge of the game, made clubs to drive down handicaps in his premises in Pilmour Place/Golf Links. Laurie passed away in 1987, but from his shop clubs go worldwide in golf bags with those privileged enough to play St Andrews.

Built in 1924 as a residence for the widow of a prominent Dundee jute baron, Rufflets has been privately owned and managed by three generations of the same family since 1952, and is one of Scotland's premier hotels.

During the night in mid August heavy transporters roll into St Andrews, and by morning the showmen are hoisting the sky-rides and unpacking the dodgems for the Lammas Fair, said to be Scotland's oldest surviving medieval market. Stalls are set up, offering all types of food, clothes and trinkets. You can win fluffy animals and, if you are brave, ascend into the sky on the stomach-churning ride with the children, who never seem to show fear. Marvel at the showmen leaping sure-footed between the sparking dodgems.

(Over page): St Andrews pipers and drummers make a braw sound as they beat and blow their way through the streets in Erskine Red tartan, ties and kilt pins displaying the motif of Saint Andrew and Scotland.

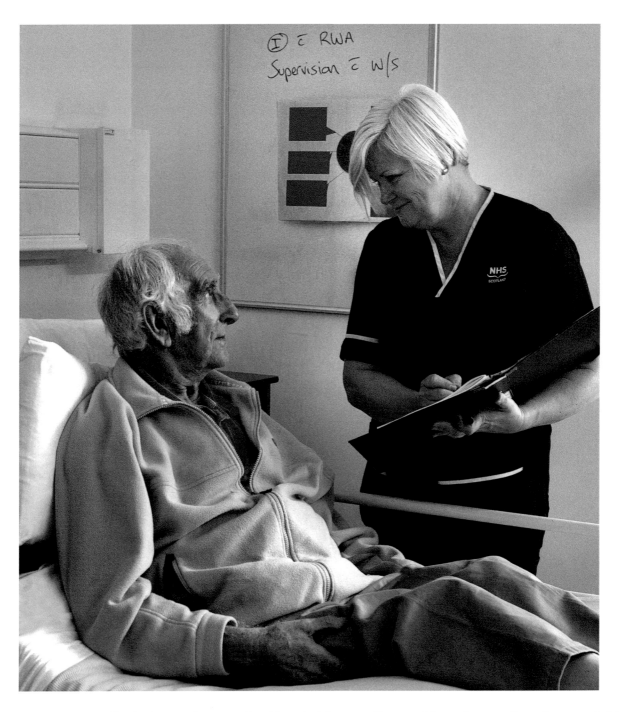

Opened in 2009, St Andrews Community Hospital has well over 90 caring staff and around 40 inpatient beds. The bright spacious building offers a wide range of services, including: GP Practices; Outpatients Department; Minor Injuries Unit and Primary Care Emergency Services Base; Renal Dialysis; Podiatry; Dentistry; Orthodontics; Physiotherapy; Rehabilitation; Community Nursing teams; Integrated Response teams and Administration services.

The Kelpies, two 30 metres tall horse heads made of steel by sculptor Andy Scott and inspired by the Scottish mythological water horse, stand alongside the Forth and Clyde Canal near Falkirk. Their maquette 'foals' were welcomed with a carnival and parade when they rode into St Andrews in July 2017. They enchanted everyone, from infants to the very elderly, who stopped to admire them at their summer stance on the Bruce Embankment, looking so real that one was tempted to feed them.

St Andrews is a city of bicycles, the majority of them belonging to students, pedalling hard towards lectures. Fortunately Spokes Cycles in South Street is there to service them. The business, started by Craig Grieve, prospered to the extent that bigger premises were required. Gordon Farquharson the manager says: 'Over the years trends have changed, one minute it's road bikes; next it's hybrids; then mountain bikes; next, road bikes. You could say it goes in cycles! The current trend is electric-assisted bikes, which enable you to keep active into your older years, or help recover from an injury, as you don't have to apply the same effort as you are assisted. Our workshop remains busy all year round and is one of the few things not affected by the internet. It is getting more difficult to compete with the internet on price, but we try to offer advice and great customer service and that personal touch that the internet can't.'

These peripatetic ducks are much-loved avian citizens of St Andrews, calling at the cycle shop, and lunching at the Subway. They visit the Barber's Pole, though they are in excellent trim.

Organised by Spokes Cycles/Limits, the Kingdom Junior Classic 2017 set out from St Andrews on Day One on the long pedal push to Falkland Hill.

'Play on pedals is the preschool, early years resource that links into the national Bikeability Scotland training programme, delivered by Cycling Scotland. By using the play on pedals games and activities the children have developed skills, balance and knowledge of bike parts and safety. At the end of the programme children who could not ride a balance bike at the start could go a balance bike with confidence and many children are starting to go pedal bikes or now confidently riding a pedal bike. I have found the programme enjoyable to use and rewarding, seeing little people riding bikes with confidence.'

Julie Clubb, Early Years Officer, Canongate School.

Football as well as golf is played with enthusiasm and skill in St Andrews. Here St Andrews United play Armadale Thistle, with victory for the home team of St Andrews at the final whistle.

'St Andrews Sailing Club was formed in 1957 and originally functioned from one of the green sheds at the side of the harbour. It then acquired the Lifeboat Shed and over the years added the floor to make two stories and the changing rooms. Lottery funding has allowed the Club to add insulation and install central heating, so the building is now used for winter talks, courses, and social events as well. We also rent the yard for boat storage from Fife Council.

Over the years we have hosted Scottish Singlehanded championships, and various traveller events for Toppers, Catamarans, Solos, GP14s. We have our annual Open Regatta, originally every June, but now changed to a more successful September date.'

Jonathon Marks, RYA Principal Instructor.

'We are basically a family-friendly club and welcome all, be they beginners or competent sailors; juniors from 9 years old to any age. There are many members who started sailing with us at a quite mature age! We aim to get you on the water and to enjoy it.'

Jonathon Marks, RYA Principal Instructor.

160

Jurek Pütter seems about to be overwhelmed by the warriors moving towards him in his creation of a St Andrews Renaissance scene, one of many such unique illustrations this brilliant artist has envisaged, after much painstaking historical research. This masterpiece hangs in the Burgh Chambers, and others adorn walls all over the world.

The Burgh of St Andrews received this exquisite gold chain from John, 3rd Marquis of Bute in 1896. Elected Rector of the University in 1892, and re-elected in 1895, this immensely wealthy and erudite coal magnate was a philanthropist who financed the Bute Medical Building. The gold chain is on display in St Andrews Museum in Kinburn House, named after the Crimean War battle of 1855.

Hugh Lyon Playfair (1787-1861), presides in the Burgh Chambers in his robes as Provost of St Andrews from 1842-61. A renaissance figure, Scottish politician, soldier and photographic pioneer, he took an abiding interest in photography during its pioneer years and worked with Sir David Brewster to develop the calotype process. He instigated many improvements in St Andrews: foot-paving the whole length of South Street; installing lighting so that the citizens could see their way home safely on dark nights; getting the harbour upgraded. He leaves his name in Playfair Terrace. Sir Hugh is buried on the north wall of St Andrews Cathedral Churchyard.

These two saxophonists are members of St Andrews and Fife Community Orchestra, conducted by Gillian Craig, which is run jointly by the University Music Centre and the Scottish Chamber Orchestra's Connect (community outreach section). Open to all players of any standard without audition, the orchestra currently numbers around 60 players who come from the local community and much further afield, this being the only orchestra of this type for miles around.

The 'Great chieftain o the puddin'-race' is led into the New Golf Club Burns Supper by Piper Duncan Soutar.

An intent admirer in the Boys' Brigade Hall watches the Fife virtuoso accordionist Billy Anderson playing a tune for a social and drill exercise evening. The St Andrews Company was formed in 1894, with the enrolment of 88 boys aged 12 years and over. Another section for boys under 12 years of age known as The Life Boys, now called the Junior Section, was formed in St Andrews in 1926. Their home is the distinctive brick hall close by the Kinness Burn.

The intrigued young lady inspects the antiquated cash register in the St Andrews shop of Aikman & Terras, when a penny bought several sweeties from a jar. The shop served the citizens of St Andrews between 1837 and 1981, but instead of its interior landing in a skip, it was reconstructed in the Preservation Trust Museum at 12 North Street, former accommodation for fisher folk, which now displays the history of St Andrews, and keeps watch on future developments so as to preserve the character of the historic city.

Though he had a home in St Andrews, Hamish McHamish preferred to spend his day roaming the streets. Chairs and food were always provided in whichever building he chose to grace with his presence. He even had his own Facebook page. When he passed away it was like the loss of a leading citizen. However, he is immortalised in bronze and in a book. This young lady cuddles his statue in Logies Lane. How long will it be until someone claims they have met his ghost padding along Market Street?

An art lover studies paintings by Francis Boag in the South Street, St Andrews gallery of Roderick and Louise Fraser. Boag has exhibited throughout the UK and also in New York, Dublin, Belfast, Paris, Munich, Michigan and Seattle. He is never without buyers.

During the summer of 2016 a mass public art trail took place around Dundee in aid of the ARCHIE Foundation Tayside, which features a series of lifelike 'Oor Wullie' sculptures, the much loved children's comic character created by the world famous D.C. Thomson of Dundee. Each 'Oor Wullie', which represented the mischievous boy sitting on his favourite place of rest, his bucket, was then given over to a variety of artists who, using their preferred medium, personalised each sculpture. One of these artists, Francis Boag chose to use his iconic lilies to decorate the sculpture, and, in a play of words, 'Oor Wullie' became 'Oor Lilies.'Oor Lily' was bought at auction by Thorntons Solicitors, when they took the colourful character on tour around schools in Tayside and North East Fife. Here, 'Oor Lily' is making a new friend at Canongate Primary School in St Andrews.

Members of the St Andrews Coastal Rowing Club pull heartily in the South Queensferry Regatta, perhaps singing a sea shanty. The Club offers both social and competitive rowing, with the less arduous kind taking place in the home waters of St Andrews Bay. More extended expeditions are undertaken from time to time, including the long haul through the Great Glen, from Banavie to Caley Marina. Who cares about blistered hands when the Club's rowers win medals regularly for speed and seamanship? The Club always welcomes new members, and anybody wishing 'taster sessions' can easily arrange them through the contacts page on the Club's website. So get in trim in the gym before you send the email.

A boat is given its colours by dedicated members of the St Andrews Coastal Rowing Club, part of the most dynamic and fastest-growing healthy leisure and community-building movement in Scotland. The St Andrews based club has more than 50 members, with an average age of 53, and has built two St Ayles skiffs, Sandbay Century and Blue Bay, and is building a smaller Wemyss skiff to give members greater flexibility and wider rowing experience. Depending on tide and weather conditions, the boats are launched from the East Sands and the St Andrews Harbour southern slipway. Outings take place on most days of the week from the early spring to the late autumn, and even continue through the winter for the hardiest and most dedicated rowers.

St Andrews Play Club staged The Ladykillers, with (left), Mike Gillan as Harry Robinson and Forbes Terris as One Round. The Play Club was formed in 1933 when the old byre of the Abbey Street Farm was leased for use as a theatre. The Play Club has performed in the Byre, off and on, to the present day.

Madras Community Dance School (M.C.D.S), currently has over 100 pupils attending dance classes. The school is run by four local teachers, who all attended the school from a young age. Founded by Carlyn Kirkcaldy in 1995, the school offers classes in various styles such as Jazz, Ballet, Highland, Cheerleading and Hip Hop for all age groups. Pupils get the opportunity to sit yearly dance exams and participate in the greatly anticipated annual dance show. Classes take place Monday to Friday Evenings and Saturday Mornings at Madras College, Kilrymont Road, St Andrews.

Ryan Stuart from the USA displays his power in the heavy events at St Andrews Highland Games, held on the last Sunday in July. The Games are a spectacle for all ages and an opportunity to show prowess as a Highland dancer, runner or cyclist.

Winter in St Andrews

'In the Beginning was the Word': a fitting message to students entering St Mary's College. The foundation was intended to have a devotional as well as an academic purpose, with daily prayers to be offered up for the respose of the soul of King James IV, slain, with knights and nobles of Scotland on 9 September 1513 on Flodden Field. This obligation, to the King's successors as well, is the reason for the royal coat of arms above the entrance.

Past Principals of St Mary's College must have trudged through the snow towards their official residence in the north-west corner of the College court, a graceful habitation from 1707 until 1978, when it was converted into offices for staff.

Snow enhances the charm of the wynds and narrow ways of St Andrews.

A monument to faith as well as to violence: the sixteenth century Dominican convent church of Blackfriars on South Street is said to have been the first building in St Andrews to have been vandalised in the Reformation, and its fragmented presence in front of Madras College reminds us what has been lost, and what might have been saved.

In the bleak midwinter Craigtoun House looks forlorn. A beer baron used to dine here, and babies were brought into the world. The large early Renaissance mansion with some Scottish Baronial features was the St Andrews seat of the Younger family. After they sold up it became a maternity hospital, functioning until 1992, when it was sold, together with 330 acres of parkland, to the Old Course Hotel, St Andrews which developed the Duke's Golf Course in the west park. The mansion is deteriorating.

Pleasing to the eye, the Romanesque-styled St Leonard's Church at Donaldson Gardens deserves a visit, particularly to stand in homage to a hero before the stained glass window, depicting 'The Lord Meeting Centurion,' by Alec Walker, 1922, with small scenes showing the healing of a servant. The window was presented by his widow in memory of Major Matthew F.M. Meiklejohn. The son of Professor John Meiklejohn of the University of St. Andrews, the Major, who was educated at Madras College, is believed to be the last soldier to have received the Victoria Cross personally from Queen Victoria, for 'conspicuous bravery' in leading soldiers of the Gordon Highlanders at the Battle of Elandslaagte on 21st October 1899 in the Boer War. He lost an arm and achieved immortality.

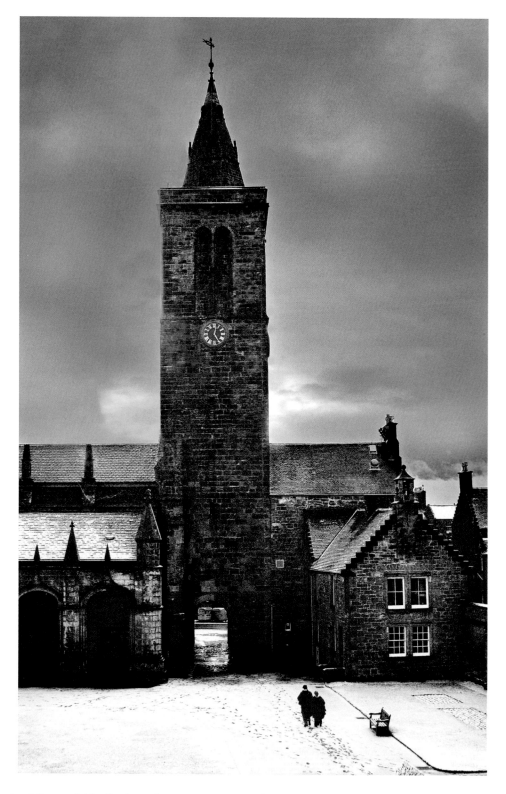

Muffled against the cold in their red gowns, two students trudge through St Salvator's Quadrangle.